The Phoenix Living Poets

SOUNDS BEFORE SLEEP

Poets Published in
The Phoenix Living Poets Series

★

JAMES AITCHISON
ALEXANDER BAIRD · ALAN BOLD
R. H. BOWDEN · FREDERICK BROADIE
GEORGE MACKAY BROWN
HAYDEN CARRUTH · JOHN COTTON
JENNIFER COUROUCLI
GLORIA EVANS DAVIES
PATRIC DICKINSON
TOM EARLEY · D. J. ENRIGHT
JOHN FULLER · DAVID GILL
PETER GRUFFYDD
J. C. HALL · MOLLY HOLDEN
JOHN HORDER · P. J. KAVANAGH
RICHARD KELL · LAURIE LEE
LAURENCE LERNER
CHRISTOPHER LEVENSON
EDWARD LOWBURY · NORMAN MACCAIG
JAMES MERRILL · RUTH MILLER
LESLIE NORRIS · ROBERT PACK
ARNOLD RATTENBURY
ADRIENNE RICH · JON SILKIN
JON STALLWORTHY
GILLIAN STONEHAM
EDWARD STOREY · TERENCE TILLER
SYDNEY TREMAYNE
LOTTE ZURNDORFER

SOUNDS
BEFORE SLEEP

by

JAMES AITCHISON

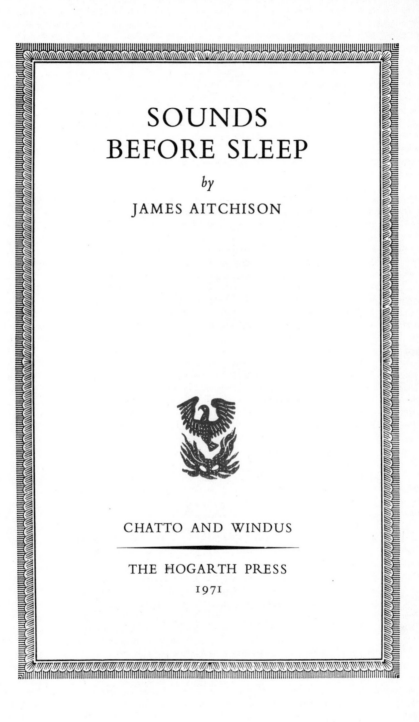

CHATTO AND WINDUS

THE HOGARTH PRESS

1971

Published by
Chatto and Windus Ltd
with The Hogarth Press Ltd
42 William IV Street
London W.C.2

★

Clarke, Irwin & Co. Ltd
Toronto

ISBN 0 7011 1761 3

Distributed in the United States of America
by Wesleyan University Press

ISBN: 0 8195 7034 6

Printed in Great Britain by
Lewis Reprints Limited
London and Tonbridge

For Norma

Some of these poems have been previously published, and grateful acknowledgment is made to the B.B.C., *Contemporary Scottish Verse, The Critical Survey, English, The Scotsman, Scottish Poetry,* and *Stand.*

Contents

March Wind

March wind is screaming through the heaving oak;
moon shines behind them, casting shadows on
our thin bedroom curtains. Half-awake,
I sense the black trees stalk across the lawn
to put their arms against the pane, to break . . .
Clouds mask the moon and the flailing arms are gone.

I watch for them, listening to them wild
in the wailing wind. I watch and hear
a new note in the screaming, a cry hurled
in terror — Nicholas. "Bad dream. Nightmare,
nasty nightmare," I whisper to my child.
And, "Hush, now, darling; sleep again, my dear."

He sleeps. In bed again, I lie awake
and listen to the shadows writhing, see
the branches scream till I know the next shriek
will be mine. I rise again, quietly,
and the house cries out at every step I take.
Downstairs, I smoke a cigarette, drink tea.

Only the wind, moonlight and March wind
in a bloody old oak tree, I try to tell
myself. But twisting noises in my mind —
the wind, the screaming branches, my son — will
not cease. I search the cabinet to find
not words this time but Equanil to still

The rushing pulses of the night. I creep
upstairs again in the creaking gloom.
The drug blurs noises and the moving shape
of the trees outside the window of our room.
In another minute I shall sleep;
tomorrow the wind might cease, and spring might come.

9

Child and Fairground

for Nicholas

He grins, climbs up and grins, begins to wave
then turns to touch the beast's chipped ears
and finger the empty socket of its eye.

Sixpence, love — she shuffles them from hand to hand
and does not see the child. The thing moves, drifts,
spills "All My Loving" across the fairground
and sails my child through the wet September evening.

Beneath scuffmarks and fading paint —
I feel the mud shift under the thin grass —
the beast is childsdream, floating, floating.

The record ends and slowly the thing
comes round again and all the beasts are still.
He grips the chipped ear and slides down
down from beast and roundabout to the soft turf.

His face is pale in the fairground lights,
all those lights and music, bells, voices, sixpences.
And I cannot hear what he says as he takes my hand.

Bonfire

for Nicholas and Caroline

A flame bursts from the fire
like a scarlet bird in flight,
hovers then disappears
in the November night.

The crimson conjurer
and all his fluttering tongues
charms the children near;
they laugh then leap back, stung

By licking flame and smoke;
firesbreath is in their cries,
and bird and crimson cloak
are burning in their eyes.

A sixpenny rocket trails
its hissing yellow arc
across the night, then fails
down through November dark.

Briefly the dry leaves flare,
the little rockets flash
faintly. The children stare
but flames have turned to ash;

The conjurer is still
and the scarlet bird is lost.
They shiver in the chill
of the November frost.

They think of sleep, they turn
towards the house and there
tonight their dreams will burn
with images of fire.

11

Hyacinth

It was the scent,
the scented weight
of those massed blooms that choked the plant.

The stem broke. Placed
in pure water,
it bleached and rotted in three days.

Pale green, grey-green,
the outer leaves
had ringed the knob of clustered buds.

The gleaming core
inside the stiff
shield swelled, yielded, began to flow.

From the moist loam
upwards slowly
the segments climbed the rising stem.

And a hundred mouths
trumpeted
their perfumed breath through the winter house.

Child and Christmas Tree

for Caroline

A dry December; sun and moonlight shine
together about your head, Caroline,

Making your beauty more than beautiful.
I rise, cross to the window, and pull

The curtains close. The tree and fairy lights
draw you, smiling, to the bauble-bright

Corner of the darkened room . . .
we need our jingling charms against the gloom,

The applause of paper unwrapped from a gift . . .
you cry and point; I rise again and lift

You up to the tree, to something far
beyond your grasp. The bell? The tinfoil star?

You smile and lean towards the star and touch . . .
tinfoil stars are just within our reach.

Morning With Mist

I cannot see where the trees begin
in this loose thicket that fills the morning,
this spillage of darkness into a day
where nothing has substance.

Slowly it silvers, begins to glint
with floating particles of freezing light
and a black stalk drifts from the iridescence
to become a tree, and a tree and a tree
until there is a far blur of woodland.

The stuff dissolves, slips, seeps away
with only a hint of frost on the wet grass
and, amongst the trees, a smear of smoke
or the breathing of some great gentle beast.

Sounds Before Sleep

I turn and turn for sleep
in the thin gasp of far gales.

I hold my breath — the gales cease
and I am lapped in the quiet tide of your breathing.

I turn and turn for sleep.
Our child stirs and cries no.
The house moans. The window shakes.

I turn and turn for sleep
and hear your hand move between the sheets
reaching from sleep to touch me, hold me.

And your warm hand stills gales.

Grandmother

In Memory of Margaret Scott Boyter

She had to steel herself to take the step
from pavement bus stop to the platform.
Inside, her wrist would stiffen as she gripped
the rail, the handbar, or some stranger's arm.

She seldom used a phone. She could not hear
the person at the other end, she said;
the line was full of noises, never clear,
and she'd ask someone else to ring instead.

We knew she felt the thing might trap, expose
her somehow; and we knew she was afraid
of voices, audible, exchanging news
of someone dying or already dead.

Night after night, when she herself was ill
she lay awake and listened to the pain
feeding on all those other fears until
a single fear was beating in her brain.

And all the other voices became one
familiar voice that whispered in her ear,
a voice that was her own yet not her own,
and softly took away the final fear.

Sunday Bus

He heaved himself into the bus and filled the aisle.
He wore a brown tweed cap, a stiff black suit.
There was a dull greased sheen on each black boot.

He sat beside me and I saw his hands,
the stained hands of an ironmoulder, such
hard hands they could have no sense of touch.

But in the corolla of his cupped hands
he held a small bunch of anemones, hid
or cherished them, violet, pink, red

Petals gleaming round the dark dark hearts.
The bus stopped. He heaved himself from his seat
and got off at the cemetery gate.

The Last Clean Bough

Each day that summer he walked the avenue
of elm and hawthorn to the broken orchard.

He put his saw to the dry boughs and he thought
of autumns full of fruit, of blossomings.

And he remembered a girl, a night when leaves
moved in the wind and moonlight silvered her.

But that was fifty years ago . . . Now
the house beyond the orchard was a shell.

The orchard wall had fallen stone by stone
and the fruitless trees had fallen: apple, plum,

Damson, cherry, pear — the pear tree where
the summer moon had found the silver girl.

The girl beneath the tree beneath the moon
was long since dead. What had they said

That summer night beneath the pear tree where
now he puts his saw to the last clean bough?

He shoulders the branch and walks the avenue
of big elms and sparse hawthorn hedge.

In his garden he drops it on the pile
of timbers stacked against the coming frost.

Early Shift, Midwinter

He knots the thong of a studded boot and wipes
his invisible footprints from the kitchen chair.

The stiffness as he straightens up, the weight
of his workboots — He has become aware

Of these things since that afternoon in March
when he shivered with cold or grief or fear

And wept beside her grave. When did he last
feel cold, shed tears or listen to a prayer?

Outside, in the blackness before dawn,
early noises stir the frozen air.

Midwinter now — less than a year. How much
did it matter that they had not shared . . .

Shared what? Each other's dreams? He did not know
what her dreams had been; he had not cared

Or thought about it till a year ago,
less than a year. And then he did not dare

Disturb her drugged oblivion. "Your wife
no longer feels the pain; you need not fear

For her." He knots the thongs of the second boot
and wipes the chair; he spits in the unlit fire

And switches off the light. Outside —
". . . no pain . . . you need not fear for her . . ." — he hears

His studded workboots ringing on the street,
early noises in the frozen air.

19

Crane Operator

He operates a Grangemouth dockyard crane.
He knows a load to a hundredweight, can guess
its clearance to within an inch. And he
knows the whine of the cable taking the strain
in that moment when the moving mass
hangs midway between the hold and quay.

Sources, voyages, arrival dates:
working with ships, he knows how vessels sail
into port, knows routes, weathers, tides
and cargoes; has learned how a deck freight
of Baltic timber in a North Sea gale
can shift, break loose, cast men over the side.

He knows cargoes: iron and bauxite ore,
cement clinker, steel slabs — the mass controlled
delicately as it bulks above
the open ship beneath. He can lower
a ton of softwood pulp to quay from hold
more tenderly than you or I make love.

House With Poplar Trees

At the far end of the towering poplar lines
his house soars. From the upper window
he oversaw his land, his farms, his mines.
He watched his poplars and his slagheaps grow.

The earth, the coal beneath the earth, the air
above, whatever breathed the air — yes, these
hirelings bonded at the yearly fair —
were his. Behind his screen of poplar trees

The place still stands today. The entrance hall
is deep in daisies, buttercups, rough grass;
the main doorway has fallen from its wall
in the crumbling remnant of the roofless house.

Nearby a dim-eyed unworked Clydesdale feeds
on what was once the lawn. You'd think a breeze
might bring the ruin down, or moss, or weeds,
behind the screen of towering poplar trees.

c

Castle At St Andrews

Even when it was whole,
it was never proof against the rush
of unleashed instincts that they called their faith,
a force that burst gates and breached walls to crush
the skulls inside, the souls
inside the flesh. They put their faith in death.

Beaton was quartered; four
lumps swung in the raw wind, daubed and stained
the broken wall in bloody heraldry.
The castle fell again, and Knox was chained
to a blistering oar;
he never ceased to prize that agony.

And so the place, fat butt
of North Sea gunners and holy attacks
of the local mobs, grew derelict.
Mortar crumbled, moss filled up the cracks.
Sound timberwork was cut
out and used again; stonemasons picked

At sandstone to redress
the damaged blocks, putting their faith and skill
into the walls of homes that would outface
the North Sea gales, ceaseless winds that chill
the other righteousness.
They made a warmly habitable place.

Doctor Bear

The gross provincial blundered — touching walls
and counting paces — into an age of elegance.
He slavered loose chewings, dribbled tea;
he tried to listen, hummed and blinked and twitched
then shouted down an age of eloquence.

Shout, shout down the skinny aesthetes! Dumb
with thunder the tinkling wits! And quell
too those melancholy doubts and fears:
that sanity's but the width of Bedlam wall,
that God might slip and list good Sam for Hell.

If he could but cry loud enough, his shout
might still be heard when he was clay.
He roared. He drank more tea and prayed and left,
counting the paces home, the paces of
'a life diversified by misery'.

Home — touching walls by cursed moonlight — home;
dear Tetty gone, and Thrale, and Garrick, gone —
testing the scrofulous mortar of his world.
Home, by damned moonlight, home to a bed
of flints, a nightsock full of scorpions.

A Corridor In Camarillo

1

And stepping into the street
he could taste the sickness that followed him
back to his room after a night at Minton's.
A phrase would turn and turn and turn and turn in his brain,
the frost formed in his wrists
and he sh.vered with fatigue yet could not sleep.

Heroin brought such warm hauntings.

2

Insomniacs prayed for sleep
or stared in silence till their fantasies
covered the ceiling from wall to trembling wall;
a sleeper stirred
and begged his serpent for another chance.
Some nights were a mad confessional
in Camarillo's ward for the withdrawn.

Outside the ward one night
he saw the arrow and the words Way Out.
It was so easy – along the corridor,
across that patch of yellow light and then . . .
And then he saw the catch –
no one could walk so far, no one would dare
those walls that flashed like blades, that final slash
of light so hot it would dissolve a man.
They found him weeping tears of laughter
in a corridor in Camarillo.

In his last winter, waiting for death
he sometimes rode the subway until dawn.
The train stopped, night people came and went
and he thought of Minton's, and remembered how
he first found the vein twenty years ago.
Between stations he stared through his own face,
already a death mask,
to the lost face of his dead child, and thought
of all the music he would never make.

The train stopped and he saw the words Way Out
and the arrow pointing along the endless corridor
as it had ten years ago. He laughed
again. Since then he'd found another way
another way. And he was almost there.

Out of the endless corridor, he dreamed
of an evening concert in the open air;
the shivering had stopped;
and as he blew
he saw the sounds as faces,
each note a child's face, floating
beneath the stars to haunt the warm night.

C*

Winter Journey

In Memory of J.B.H.

So much space . . . Christmas in Ealing
and they'd forgotten there was so much space.
After the long term
they had forgotten there were days like this
when winter sunlight on the frozen fields
picked out a gleam of frost along each twig
each blade of grass and on the dozen dead
moles iced to the roadside fence
as they drove northwards into Yorkshire.

It was the sun of course,
it was the angle of midwinter sun
meeting frost on the fields and snow on the rising moors.
They had forgotten days like this
and they laughed at so much space, so much light.
Between terms, with seven more days
and no rehearsals, no rehearsals —
hardly a need for words on a day like this.
Had they really forgotten, he wondered,
or was this perhaps the first day they had shared?
The car veered as they kissed and laughed at so much space.

They drove through Yorkshire and the turning day
when late sun and full moon lit the moorland snow,
like Christmas Eve again, like the journey down;
turn of the year and now the journey home
to a house full of Christmas cards
and seven more days before he turned to words
again, to all those words;
turn of a road where fence posts and thorn hedge
grew across the fields, climbed the hillside
and disappeared in the upland snow.
There are no boundaries on the high moors.

26

And he laughed at so much space, so much light,
laughed as he turned to kiss in a last
sublime absentmindedness.
Turn in the road, a patch of ice in a dip,
another bend, sharper, and those headlights suddenly huge —
a wild implosion of laughter and light and space.
Near Richmond . . . there are many mansions . . .
instantly . . . they didn't have a chance . . .
to find a nightingale . . . to open Christmas cards . . .
near Richmond . . . if it were not so . . . instantly . . .
I would have told you . . . near Richmond . . . instantly.

And he laughed and laughed at so much light and space.

Citizen 5 6 3 4 8

Did it show, he wondered, when a word
they had deleted slid into his mind?
No, not possible; no, it was absurd.
But the word stuck to his tongue. Might he not find
the sudden heartbeat could be overheard?

The little man who asked him for a light
that morning called him friend and made a joke
about the president. He had to bite
back the smile from his shut lips. Men who spoke
like that might come back quietly in the night.

White waters reaching up a warm shore —
he'd heard or overheard someone saying
it was like that. But he knew that the whore
beneath him on the bed was listening
for footsteps, voices, fists on the outer door.

At night he dreamed of burning till the heat
woke him. He sat up and struck a match
and thought of the little man who joked. Sweat
cooled and he crossed to the window to watch
policemen in pairs patrol the empty street.

Down there in a few hours more, among
the thousands who would look once and then walk
on, the man who joked might come along
with other men, invite him for a talk
and see the marks of burning on his tongue.

A Woman's Place

The bluebottle,
sated with offal and satin-shiny with filth,
droned above the new pram in the garden,
hovered, hovered
and settled on the sleeping baby's brow.
It printed its microscopic steps of dirt
down into the corner of a closed eye, where
it fastidiously rubbed the offal from its hands
and rinsed and rinsed its hair-thin filthy wrists.

A merest nerve
in the immaculate eyelid of the sleeping child
twitched, twitched
and eyes and mouth and minute nostrils flared
crimson as it screamed itself awake,
hurled its terrified screaming at the house
in its incredible terror of first fear.
The insect kissed eyelashes, nostrils, lips.

Pink-faced,
the mother paused and blinked in the steam that rose
from a sinkful of breakfast crockery,
listened, pierced by the screaming of her flesh,
her flesh — but these chores
and then that pile of yesterday's soiled clothes
to wash and then the airing, ironing
and flustered shopping from some passing vans
and cooking, cleaning, clearing up against
the chaos that might break at any hour.

An hour like this.
She turned to look at the kitchen clock,
its ticking silenced by the baby's fear —
her flesh, her chaos —
turned again to the items in the sink
and rubbed and rubbed at the half-seen crockery.

Off Season

You mean you're here the whole year round, she said.
How nice, she said. But don't you sometimes find . . .
I mean, an old . . . an older man like you,
don't you feel . . . I mean, the whole year round.
And what she meant was surely you must have thought
of gas or drowning or an overdose.
And it's so cold in winter here, she said.

Cold, but in winter the place was his.
He listened to his footsteps on the stairs
like daily music, and across the hall;
and every morning when he closed the door
heard echoes in the empty rooms.

Better without them, the summer visitors
who sniggered in the night. They never saw
frost in the hedges of felt the chill
taste of sea mist, thinning now, like this.
The place was best off-season, he thought,
the funfair boarded up and spangled with birdshit,
the sands stiff and grey with frost and
the empty beach awash with pale sea mist.

Better without them. Oh, they're nice enough,
he thought, until you try to talk to them
or to their children. Let an old man speak
childish secrets to a child and see
the fear and hatred in the parent's eyes.

And he remembered thinking of it once,
of walking down a beach
through the mist and into the winter sea.
But that was years ago. And now there were
only his footprints in the frosted sand

and nothing could be lovelier than this
December morning with a hint of sun
and sea mist shrinking back into the sea.

And In The Silences

And in the silences —
when she holds a cup against her lips
but does not drink, or when it seems to slip
her mind that he is with her in the room —
he sees her face assume
the new configuration, with a trace
of time around the eyes, the little lines
suggesting distances
or sounding depths where days have quietly drowned.

A world has fallen from her fingertips
and will not now be found.
And in those instances
he looks and wishes that he could replace
the dream that time consumes;
yet through the silences —
reading between the lines —
he also sees how the lost dream defines
a new dimension of her loveliness
as beauty grows into a daily grace.